KW-179-389

Contents

Chairman's Foreword

To: The Rt Hon Jack Straw MP, Lord Chancellor and Secretary of State for Justice. Submitted in accordance with Schedule 1 to the Criminal Appeal Act 1995.

The far-reaching internal reorganisation and reform of our processes, to which I referred last year, began to deliver the positive results we had envisaged and hoped for. There have been dramatic reductions in waiting times, as the figures elsewhere in this report demonstrate, despite a reduction in the number of case reviewers resulting from budgetary pressures. Thus, this is not only a vindication of the changes we have introduced, but a resounding tribute to our staff whose commitment and energy I salute. The executive directors have carried a heavy burden and given unstinting support.

In these circumstances, the Commissioners and I are particularly sad that the Treasury guidelines on pay have required us (because progression and annual increments have to be included) to offer a pay award this year which falls so far short of inflation that most are experiencing a real cut in pay. We recognise the need for pay restraint in the public sector but when two-thirds of our staff receive an award of only 1.2%, it is easy to see why we feel frustrated and the staff feel angry and dispirited.

Our pleasure at the impact of the new arrangements on waiting times is tempered by the knowledge that these gains which have been secured through so much effort are unlikely to be sustained if the proposed budget reductions of £100k in money terms for each of the next three years are confirmed. A reduction of this order, equivalent in real terms to a reduction amounting to around £300,000 per annum once inflation is taken into account, will mean that staff numbers will have to continue to fall. Indeed, our inability to fill vacancies in anticipation of these reductions – our complement of case review managers has dropped by almost 10% over the year – is already reversing these improvements. The one thing we are not prepared to do is to compromise the quality or intensity of our reviews. We have made significant economies and will continue to do so wherever possible, but there is now minimal scope for savings which will not damage the quality and efficiency of our work.

There were two aspects of our operation which for some time officials had been suggesting should be modified so as to cut costs. One was the treatment of applications in which the applicant had not previously appealed and the other was our practice of requiring that a Commissioner, and not a member of staff, should take any final decision not to refer a case. We reconsidered our position in respect of both these matters from first principles as a result of which we reaffirmed our practice and produced detailed reports for consideration by officials, not because it was for them to dictate our internal procedures but because we acknowledge that they (on your behalf) are entitled to raise issues with us which ultimately involve value for money. I am pleased to say that our two reports satisfied your officials that our policy in these two areas was appropriate on legal, policy and financial grounds.

We marked, and indeed celebrated, our tenth anniversary by holding an international conference on miscarriages of justice in May 2007 together with the Institute of Judicial Administration at the University of Birmingham's School of Law. Our speakers included the President of the Queen's Bench Division, the Director of Public Prosecutions, a former Minister of Justice and Attorney General of Canada, the founder of the Innocence Project in the USA, the Shadow Attorney General and the Director of Liberty. The Senior Law Lord, who was Lord Chief Justice at the time of the creation of the Commission and during its early years, spoke at the post-conference dinner.

It is rare for convictions we have referred to the Court of Appeal to find their way to the House of Lords, but this has happened twice in the past year and in both cases the Appellate Committee reversed the

Court of Appeal and quashed the convictions[1], in effect affirming the Commission's understanding of the law and illustrating the inherent difficulty in predicting, as the statutory test requires us to do, how the courts will decide the cases we review. We also have to pick up the consequences of any House of Lords decisions in other criminal cases where the criminal law is in effect changed, such as *Coutts* [2006] UKHL 39 and *Wang* [2005] UKHL 9 which caused us to examine or re-examine applications and place appeals before the Court of Appeal[2].

This possibility arises because the common law to be taken into account when reviewing a conviction is the law at the time of the review and not as at the date of conviction. I referred to this last year, when I wrote that "A resounding affirmation of the Commission's independence came from the Divisional Court when it rejected an attempt by the Director of the Revenue and Customs Prosecution Office… to seek judicial review of a number of referrals to the Court of Appeal". I noted that the Divisional Court's judgment was being questioned by the Court of Appeal, which in the event purported to limit its ambit by stating that the Commission was bound to take into account the Court's own practice in considering applications for extension of time in which to appeal on the basis of a development in the law[3], which in fact was already the Commission's policy. Parliament has now intervened and the Criminal Justice and Immigration Act 2008 has added a new section to the Criminal Appeal Act 1968 which allows the Court, on a reference by us, to disregard any development in the law if it is one in respect of which it would not itself have granted leave.

This is the last annual report that I shall have the honour to submit. I complete my term of office half way through the next Commission year. It has been a singular privilege to chair this organisation, which in its 11-year life has so successfully established itself as an indispensable feature of the legal landscape. As the Lord Chief Justice commented in his Introduction to the Court of Appeal, Criminal Division's Review of the Legal Year 2006/2007: "The Commission performs invaluable work. In relation to some appeals it has become virtually the investigative arm of the Court itself. As with the Court, one may well ask how the criminal justice system managed without it."

In the Review itself, the section dealing with the Commission concludes: "It is hoped that the Court's unique relationship with the CCRC will continue to develop over future years, to achieve our mutual goal of a criminal justice system that is capable of recognising and rectifying potential miscarriages of justice when they occur."

I wish my successor (as yet unappointed) every success at the head of an organisation which plays a crucial role in helping to secure justice and which rightly commands international attention and admiration. He or she will inherit a united and supportive group of Commissioners, a skilled and dedicated staff, and an organisation far more self-critical than it once was, together with the melancholic challenges which spring from proposed reductions to our budget which would be as damaging in practice as they are demoralising in prospect.

Graham Zellick

[1] *Kennedy* [2007] UKHL 38; *Clarke and McDaid* [2008] UKHL 8: see further p17 below.
[2] See p17 below.
[3] *Cottrell and Fletcher* [2007] EWCA Crim 2016

The year in numbers

In 2007-08:

984

applications were received, compared with 1,051 last year.

1,087

cases were completed, compared with 990 last year.

450

cases were under review as at 31 March 2008, compared with 464 as at 31 March 2007.

194

cases were awaiting allocation (compared to 283 as at 31 March 2007). Of these, 112 had been categorised and were waiting to be allocated for review. The remainder were in the process of being prepared and categorised, or were new applications just received.

27

cases were referred to the appeal courts (compared with 38 last year).

2.5%

of completed cases were referred to the appeal courts. This figure fluctuates from year to year, but the overall referral rate since the Commission was set up in 1997 is 3.8%.

65%

of Commission referrals heard by the appeal courts resulted in convictions being quashed or sentences varied. A total of 46 referrals were heard by the appeal courts and of these, 30 convictions were quashed or sentences varied.

Section
One

Management
Commentary

Directors' Report

History

The Commission was established on 1 January 1997 by the Criminal Appeal Act 1995 (hereafter referred to as 'the Act'). From 31 March 1997, the Commission assumed the responsibilities for reviewing possible miscarriages of justice previously exercised by the Home Office and the Northern Ireland Office. The Commission is based in Birmingham.

Statutory background

The Commission transferred with its sponsor unit, the Office for Criminal Justice Reform, from the Home Office to the new Ministry of Justice on 9 May 2007. As at 31 March 2008, the Commission was an Executive Non-Departmental Public Body financed by Grant in Aid through the Ministry of Justice Main Estimate. The Lord Chancellor and Secretary of State for Justice is answerable to Parliament for the Commission and responsible for making financial provision to meet its needs. The Secretary of State for Northern Ireland has similar responsibilities in respect of Northern Ireland. The Act provides that the Commission shall have no fewer than 11 Commissioners, appointed by The Queen on the recommendation of the Prime Minister, one of whom is appointed by The Queen as Chairman.

Principal activities

The Commission carries out the following functions as set out in the Act:

- To refer a conviction, verdict, finding or sentence to an appropriate court of appeal when it considers that there is a real possibility that it would not be upheld (sections 9-12)
- To investigate and report to the Court of Appeal on any matter on which it is directed by the Court to investigate and report (section 15)
- To consider any reference from the Secretary of State of any matters in relation to the royal prerogative of mercy, and to give a statement of its conclusions (section 16(1))
- To give reasons for its opinion in any case where it determines that the Secretary of State should consider recommending an exercise of the prerogative of mercy (under section 16(2)).

Commissioners and directors

Commissioners

Commissioners are appointed for up to five years by The Queen on the recommendation of the Prime Minister. Commissioners meet regularly to review and decide on the Commission's policies, performance and other issues of strategic importance. Directors are in attendance at these meetings. During the year 2007-08, the Commissioners were:

Professor Graham Zellick (Chairman)
Mr Michael Allen
Ms Penelope Barrett
Mr Mark Emerton
Mr James England
Miss Julie Goulding
Mr David Jessel

Mr Alastair MacGregor QC (Deputy Chairman)
Mr Ian Nichol
Mr Ewen Smith
Mr John Weeden CB

Directors

The day-to-day running of the Commission is the responsibility of the Directors, who together comprise the Senior Management Team. During the year, the Directors were:

Mr Colin Albert, Principal Director and Director of Finance & IT (and Accounting Officer)
Miss Karen Kneller, Director of Casework.

Code of Best Practice

The Commission adopted a Code of Best Practice for Commissioners at its first meeting in January 1997 and undertook to review it annually. The Commission adopted a revised Code of Best Practice for Commissioners in January 2004. The Commission's Code of Best Practice includes a register of Commissioners' interests which is available for inspection at the Commission by arrangement.

Risks and uncertainties

The Commission's systems of internal control have been designed to manage the risks the Commission faces, to safeguard its assets against unauthorised use or disposition, to maintain proper accounting records and to communicate reliable information for internal use or publication.

Audit Committee

This ensures high standards of financial reporting and systems of internal control and reporting procedures. It reviews internal and external financial statements on behalf of the Commission. Chairman: Mr Terry Price (external).

Auditor

Arrangements for external audit are provided under paragraph 9 of Schedule 1 to the Act, which requires the Comptroller and Auditor General to examine, certify and report on the statement of accounts. His report, together with the accounts, is laid before each House of Parliament.

No remuneration was paid to the auditor for non-audit work during the year. As far as the Accounting Officer is aware, there is no relevant audit information of which the Commission's auditor is unaware. The Accounting Officer has taken all the steps which he ought to have taken to make himself aware of any relevant audit information and to establish that the Commission's auditor is aware of that information.

Personal data related incidents

There were no personal data related incidents in the year, or in any previous year, which had to be reported to the Information Commissioner or were otherwise recorded as being of significance.

The Commission takes great care to protect personal data relating to applicants, witnesses, victims and others connected with cases under review, and section 23 of the Criminal Appeal Act 1995 makes it an offence to disclose any information obtained by the Commission in the exercise of its functions except in very specific circumstances. The Commission will be undertaking a review of its information risks in the forthcoming year to ensure that any weaknesses that may exist are identified and appropriate action taken.

Other reportable matters
In respect of the year ended 31 March 2008:

- No research and development was undertaken
- No donations to charity were made
- There are no post-balance sheet events to report

How we work

The case review process
The Commission reviews cases by:

- Using its own resources and expertise (for example, case reviewers and Legal and Investigations Advisers)
- Using its powers under section 17 of the Criminal Appeal Act to obtain relevant material held by public bodies
- Commissioning outside experts to prepare reports
- Requiring the appointment of an Investigating Officer under section 19 of the Act.

At the end of every review, Commissioners decide if the case should be referred to the relevant appeal court or not. A single Commissioner can decide not to refer a case but (as prescribed in the Act) only a committee of at least three Commissioners can decide to refer a case.

If a case is referred, the applicant is sent a Statement of Reasons setting out the reasons for the decision. The appeal court and prosecuting authority also receive a copy.

If a provisional view is reached not to refer the case, the applicant is sent a Provisional Statement of Reasons explaining the reasons. Applicants are given time to make further representations if they wish. These are considered before a decision is made and a final Statement of Reasons is issued.

The review process involves:

Stage 1
Applications arrive and are assessed for eligibility. The Commission will not review a case where the applicant is in the process of appealing and these are closed. If the applicant has not appealed, a Commissioner will consider whether (i) there is a real possibility that an appeal would succeed or that an investigation might give rise to such a real possibility; and

(ii) whether there might be exceptional circumstances (as required by the Act where there has been no previous appeal) to justify a referral. If the answers to both (i) and (ii) are yes, the case will be categorised for review in the normal way. Otherwise, the Commissioner will issue a provisional view in letter format to the applicant or representative, allowing 28 days for further submissions. If no further submissions are received, or if submissions are received but they do not alter the Commissioner's opinion, the Commissioner will close the case and issue a final letter to the applicant or representative. If the further submissions persuade the Commissioner that the answers to (i) and (ii) are yes, the case will be categorised for review in the normal way.

If an applicant re-applies to the Commission, a Commissioner who took no part in any previous application will determine whether or not anything new is being raised that justifies a further review. If not, the application will not be accepted. Cases where there are no reviewable grounds (for example, where the application form is blank, or all of the submissions clearly repeat issues already considered at trial or by the appeal court) are dealt with by Commissioners who will send a provisional view. The applicant will be given 28 days to respond, after which either the application will be categorised as a review case or a final decision not to refer will be issued.

For cases accepted for review, the Commissioner at Stage 1 will categorise the case according to its complexity and work content. Initial consideration by a Commissioner, for the purpose of case categorisation, will include an assessment of the application having regard to the submissions and all relevant documents.

Review cases
Each case is allocated to a case reviewer. Cases are divided into four categories:

Category A
These are typically straightforward or raise issues which can be addressed thoroughly on the available case papers and are unlikely to involve complex points of law. They should normally be capable of being reviewed and passed to the decision-making stage within eight weeks of allocation.

Category B
These are more involved and typically raise issues of some complexity, possibly with extensive material to review or the likely involvement of another agency. They are expected to be ready to go to the decision-making stage within 22 weeks of allocation.

Category C
These are likely to require a more time-consuming review and typically the issues are extensive and complex, possibly requiring wide-ranging off-site enquiries or the input of other agencies. A Commissioner will be assigned to each C case to help the case reviewer plan and execute the review. There will be a Case Planning Committee in all C cases, which will set the target date for completion.

Category D

These are exceptional cases which are referred to the Director of Casework when received. For example, they may be extremely large cases or ones in which the need for a section 19 investigation is evident from the outset. Once the appropriate approach has been decided, Category D cases will normally be assigned to and follow one of the A, B or C pathways for the review.

The above milestones relate to bringing the review to a point where the case is ready to go to a Commissioner or a committee of Commissioners for a decision to be made. Separate timetables apply to the decision-making phase and these may be affected by external factors such as, in the case of a provisional decision not to refer, the volume, complexity and timeliness of further representations received in response. In the case of a referral, factors such as preparation of material for disclosure with the decision, or notifying affected parties, may affect the timetable.

Case ordering and priority ranking

Most cases are dealt with in order of receipt. Category B and C cases, which are more time-consuming, wait in separate queues. B and C cases where the applicant is in custody are prioritised over cases where the applicant is at liberty. Factors such as the age and health of applicants and witnesses, and the possibility of deterioration of evidence, are taken into account. Priority may also be assigned to cases of particular significance to the criminal justice system where, for example, public confidence is an issue.

Review of the year and performance

The following strategic aims guided our work over the year:

1. Casework: To review cases efficiently and effectively and with the minimum of delay consistent with the circumstances of individual cases.
2. Resources: To ensure that the core activities of the Commission were supported by the appropriate use of available resources and that value for money was delivered.
3. Corporate: To ensure that the Commission's activities were properly planned and monitored, that it achieved an appropriate public profile, and that a positive contribution to the criminal justice system was made.

Casework

Summary

Last year we reported on the new processes and structures implemented in 2006-07 following an internal review conducted by the Commission with the help of consultants. This year was the first full year operating the new processes, but already those changes to casework processes started to take effect, bringing some quite dramatic improvements.

There were significant improvements over the year in cutting waiting-times for cases to be allocated for review, with waiting-times improving by around 12 months across the board for those cases requiring a more time consuming review (category B and C cases). There was a substantial reduction in the number of cases waiting to be allocated, with 194 waiting at the end of the year, compared with 283 the previous year. Only 66 of the cases waiting were B and C cases.

The Commission closed 1,087 cases against an intake of 984 - 103 cases more than it received. This is an excellent result and compares with closing 61 cases fewer than it received in 2006-07.

Completing an acceptable number of cases within our benchmark timescales has remained a challenge, largely as a result of old, complex cases still in the system from before the changes to casework processes. This will be a key focus of our efforts for 2008-09.

Cases in progress
It is important that we complete case reviews in a reasonable time. We measure this only for B and C cases as these cases take much longer to review than category A cases. For B cases we had 31 cases (at 31 March 2008) which had yet to reach the provisional decision stage and which were allocated more than six months earlier (above the target of fewer than 20 cases set out in our Key Performance Indicator 1 (see page 31)). However, although the number of cases was higher than we would like, their average age (at less than 12 months) was only slightly above the target of less than 10 months. For C cases, the picture was reversed, with the actual number of cases very close to the target (30 cases against a target of fewer than 30 cases) but the average age in excess of target.

Age of next case for allocation
We have recognised that one of the main concerns for applicants is the length of time they must wait before their case is allocated for review. This is an area in which the Commission has performed significantly better this year than in previous years. Our performance on Key Performance Indicator 2 (see page 31) gives an indication of this as it measures the average age in months of all review cases not yet allocated and the age in months of the next case to be allocated. This is shown separately for in-custody and at-liberty cases for category B and C cases.

For A cases, the age of the next case to be allocated (at 31 March 2008) was five months, which was just shy of meeting the planned milestone of less than five months. For B in-custody cases, the age of the next case was five months, well within the plan of nine months. For B at-liberty cases, again, the age of the next case to be allocated was, at 16 months old, within the plan of fewer than 21 months. For C cases, the trend continued with the age of the next C in-custody case to be allocated at six months, well within the target of 16 months. C at-liberty cases have also performed well, with the age of the next case 17 months, comfortably within the target of 28 months. The average age of cases waiting is within our milestone values for all types of cases except A cases, for which the average age is 3.07 months, marginally in excess of the milestone of 3 months. Nevertheless, average waiting times have improved significantly over the year.

Case completion times
It is also important that, once a review has begun, cases are completed within a reasonable time. Key Performance Indicator 3 (see page 32) measures the number of cases which reach the provisional statement of reasons stage and the final decision stage within our benchmark times expressed as a percentage of all cases. Case completion times for C cases are within target, although it is significant that the margin is less for the final decision than for the provisional, mainly as a result of dealing with additional representations from

applicants once a provisional decision has been communicated. For category A and B cases completion times have exceeded target, and this will form the focus of our efforts in the ensuing year.

Caseflow balance

If the Commission closes cases efficiently and overall case closures exceed the intake of cases, our backlogs will be eroded. If we close fewer cases than we receive, the number of cases waiting to be allocated for review will increase and the waiting times to allocation will grow. This year our aim, as set out in Key Performance Indicator 4 (see page 32), was to close more cases than we received and our performance was excellent, closing 103 more cases than we received. Although we received 67 fewer applications in 2007-08 than in 2006-07, this improved performance was not just a result of the lower intake, as we closed 97 more cases in 2007-08 than in 2006-07. This had a positive impact on the number of cases waiting and waiting-times.

As reported at the beginning of this chapter, the Commission has seen dramatic improvements in the number of cases waiting to be allocated for review and a dramatic fall in those waiting times. Whilst the new processes and structures have provided the foundation for those dramatic improvements, there is no doubt that this would not have been possible without the dedicated efforts of staff and Commissioners.

The challenge for next year will be to maintain this position in light of significant budget reductions and a consequent freeze on the appointment of new case reviewers to replace those who have left during 2007-08 and those who may leave in 2008-09.

Applications received v cases closed

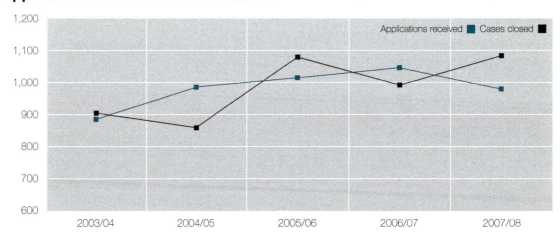

Referrals

This year the Commission referred 28 cases to the appeal courts, which represents 2.6% of the 1,087 cases completed over the year. As at 31 March 2008, the Commission had referred 384 out of 10,038 cases completed since our creation, an overall referral rate of 3.8%.

Referral conclusions

The proportion of referrals which result in a conviction being quashed or a sentence varied is a measure of our interpretation of the 'real possibility' test. This year the appeal courts delivered judgments in 46 of our referrals, quashing or varying 30 (65%). This was within our forecast of 60-80%, as set out in Key Performance Indicator 6 (see page 33). As at 31 March 2008, the appeal courts, including the House of Lords, had determined a total of 357 referrals since the Commission's inception, quashing 211 convictions (67% of those referred) and upholding 102 (33%). 39 sentences had been varied (89% of those referred) and five upheld (11%).

The combined rate of convictions quashed and sentences varied since the Commission began is 70%.

Referrals as % of cases closed

Average: 3.83%

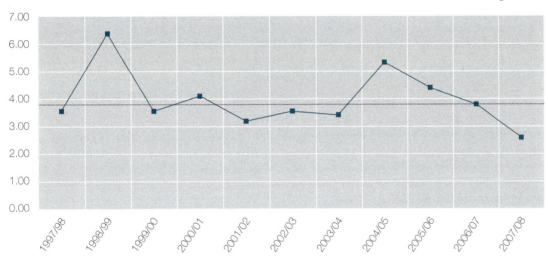

Outcome of referrals heard

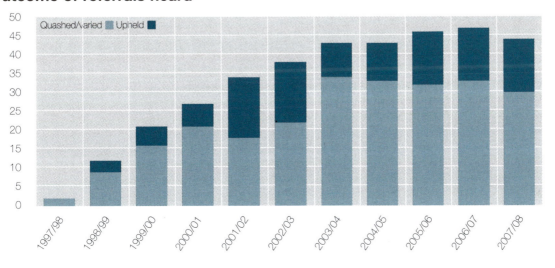

Analysis of Commission references to the appeal courts in 2007-08
(see table 1 on page 28)
During the period covered by this report, the Commission referred to the appeal courts cases involving 27 individual appellants: 22 of these references related to convictions and five concerned sentences (one of them a summary matter).

As at 31 March 2008, nine had had their conviction quashed or sentence varied and three had been upheld. None of the remaining references have yet been heard.

Seven referrals were in relation to sexual offences, seven cases can broadly be categorised as involving the use of non-fatal force and six references were made in relation to murder (including attempted murder and conspiracy to murder). There were two people whose cases concerned dishonesty and only one who had been convicted of a drugs offence. This is in sharp contrast to the previous year, when the cases of 15 individuals were referred in connection with the importation and supply of controlled drugs. Those who feared that the Court of Appeal might be inundated by a flood of references arising from the handling of informants in such cases (see our Annual Reports for the previous two years) have not seen their predictions fulfilled. The Commission is regularly said to have opened one set of floodgates or another, but in reality no unmanageable deluge has yet materialised on any of these occasions.

Themes
The complexity of recent sentencing legislation continued to feature in references. In particular, the case of *R v Giga* [2008] EWCA Crim 703 which was referred in February 2008, provided the Court of Appeal with an opportunity to consider whether a sentencing judge's misinterpretation of the early-release provisions should prompt any adjustment of an otherwise acceptable sentence.

Last year's Annual Report remarked on cases that were referred because of fresh evidence suggesting that complainants in sexual offences may have been less reliable than they appeared to the jury. This theme has continued, and the majority of the references made in sexual cases were based on similar concerns.

In a return to a theme from the earlier years of the Commission's existence, three connected convictions from the mid-1980s were referred because of concern about the reliability of confessions made by young people.

Analysis of the decisions by the appeal courts in 2007-08
(see table 2 on page 29)
The appeal courts decided the cases of 46 individuals referred by the Commission. 41 were heard by the Court of Appeal, Criminal Division, in London, one in the Northern Ireland Court of Appeal and three in the House of Lords. The remaining matter was a summary appeal heard in the Crown Court.

This year, only seven of the references related to homicide, compared with 15 last year; 12 concerned sexual offences; 14 involved supplying or importing drugs; three concerned dishonesty; four involved non-fatal violence; and four were about money-laundering. The summary matter was about a dangerous dog.

The appeal courts decided that 24 of the 40 convictions referred by the Commission were unsafe. Sixteen of the appeals were dismissed, including one which was abandoned by the applicant. Of the six sentences referred, all were reduced.

Themes

Although our work is often only seen in terms of the human dramas at the centre of individual cases, this year has provided several examples of the way that Commission references can contribute to the much broader development of legal principles.

Unusually, the House of Lords examined a Commission reference in which the conviction had been upheld by the Court of Appeal. We had found two lines of authority in the Court of Appeal, giving different outcomes in cases where an appellant had assisted someone else to inject drugs from which the drug-user had died. One line held the appellant liable for 'unlawful act' manslaughter, but the House of Lords preferred to follow the other line and in doing so reversed the Court of Appeal, holding that the user's own act of injecting himself with the drug had broken the chain of causation which linked the appellant legally to the death (*R v Kennedy* [2007] UKHL 38).

Still in the area of the law on homicide (a subject which was receiving close attention during the year in the wake of the Law Commission's 2006 report *Murder, Manslaughter and Infanticide*), our reference of an infanticide conviction caused some controversy among lawyers. *R v Gore* [2007] EWCA Crim 2789 raised the question of whether it was necessary for a woman to have an intention to kill or seriously injure her baby before she could be guilty of infanticide. In a controversial judgment that was critical of the Commission, the Court of Appeal held that infanticide was not a sub-category of murder, and therefore one could be guilty of the offence as a result of any deliberate act or omission, however well-intended it may have been, if one's baby died as a consequence.

Last year's Annual Report mentioned the Court of Appeal's decision to uphold the convictions in *R v Clarke & McDaid* [2006] EWCA Crim 1196, referred by us for want of a signature on the indictment. Although apparently a mere technicality, the House of Lords reversed the Court of Appeal and quashed the conviction ([2008] UKHL 8).

Moving to broader issues, the Commission contributed two references to a group of four appeals heard together in order to clarify when judges should allow juries to consider the possibility of convicting defendants of some less serious offence than the one for which they were standing trial (*R v Foster and others* [2007] EWCA Crim 2869), following the earlier House of Lords decision in *R v Coutts* [2006] UKHL 39.

Change of law – that is, when the case law changes after the date of conviction and appeal, which then is the law that both the Commission and the Court of Appeal must apply – was one of last year's themes, following the referral of several convictions in the light of the House of Lords' decision in the money-laundering case of *Saik* [2006] UKHL 18. The Divisional Court was asked by the prosecutor in judicial review proceedings to rule that the Commission should refer only if the Court of Appeal would itself have granted leave to appeal out of time in such a case. The Divisional Court held that the Commission was under no such obligation (*R (Director of Revenue and Customs Prosecution) v CCRC* [2007] 1

CrAppR 384), but the Court of Appeal in a later case expressed the view that the Commission was obliged to have regard to the Court's practice not to allow an extension of time based on a change in the law unless there had been substantial injustice (*Cottrell and Fletcher* [2007] EWCA Crim 2016). What particularly troubled the Court was that, once such a case had been referred, the Court had to apply the new law and if it rendered the conviction unsafe had no choice but to quash the conviction, even if it were a case in which they would not themselves have granted leave to appeal. This problem has now been addressed by section 42 of the Criminal Justice and Immigration Act 2008.

The decision which attracted most attention from the media was one which recalled another familiar theme, that of expert evidence. Barry George's conviction for the murder of Jill Dando was quashed in November 2007 (and a retrial was ordered) because of refinements in the way that the Forensic Science Service expressed the significance of microscopic traces of firearms residue (*R v George* [2007] EWCA Crim 2722).

Northern Ireland
The casework statistics presented so far combine England, Wales and Northern Ireland. Cases from Northern Ireland for the period 31 March 1997 to 31 March 2008 show a different pattern from those in England and Wales, with higher referral and quashing rates. Of the 161 applications by 31 March 2008, 123 had been closed, resulting in 18 referrals (15%). Fourteen convictions had been quashed (87.5%) and two (12.5%) upheld, with two cases still to be heard at 31 March 2008.

Directions for investigation by the Court of Appeal
The Commission can be directed to investigate and report on matters referred to it by the Court of Appeal under section 23A of the Criminal Appeal Act 1968 and section 15 of the Criminal Appeal Act 1995. We continue to have a steady number of these cases, with 11 received this year (the same as last year). Because they relate to live proceedings, they are always given priority and continue to occupy a significant amount of investigation time. A continuing theme was enquiries relating to jury contamination or bias. As the Court of Appeal noted in its annual report for 2006/07, it "has been extremely grateful for the prompt and thorough response of the CCRC in each case" (para 4.7). The Court also observed that our status as an independent body "instils public confidence in these investigations" (para 4.9).

The prerogative of mercy
The Secretary of State's power, under section 16 of the Act, to seek the Commission's advice in relation to recommendations concerning the prerogative of mercy has never been used; nor has the Commission exercised its own power under the section to make any such recommendations to the Secretary of State.

During the year the Secretary of State asked the Commission to advise him on the exercise of his power to refer a conviction to the Jersey Court of Appeal. This is not covered by our statutory powers and, although we offered advice in this case, it would be better if the three

UK Crown Dependencies (Jersey, Guernsey and the Isle of Man) were brought within the Commission's remit.

Complaints and judicial reviews

The Complaints Manager considers complaints and carries out a detailed investigation if necessary, working within the complaints procedure. Dissatisfied complainants can apply for a review of their complaint by the Chairman or his nominee.

The Commission is not subject to the Parliamentary Ombudsman, a position which was originally recommended in the Royal Commission report which led to our creation and has recently been reaffirmed.[1]

In 2007-08, we received 40 complaints (compared with 39 in 2006-07). There were four complaints outstanding from the previous year. A total of 41 complaints were resolved during the year, leaving three complaints outstanding. No cases were re-opened, although three complaints were partially upheld on the basis of failure to correspond adequately and a minor disclosure error.

During the year, the Commission was the subject of 30 separate applications for judicial review of its case-related decisions. The vast majority of these challenges focused on the Commission's conclusion that there was no real possibility that the conviction would be quashed. Five ended during the pre-action exchange of correspondence: in two of these cases we recognised that our investigation or reasoning had fallen short of what we felt was appropriate, and those cases were reconsidered; in the other three no applications were ever submitted to the Administrative Court.

The Administrative Court refused permission to proceed in 12 cases where claims were lodged with the Court, and one was discontinued by the claimant because of his poor health.

Permission for judicial review was granted in three cases (equalling 14% of the 21 judicial reviews and pre-protocol letters completed).

In one, we agreed to conduct a further review in relation to some pathological evidence. Another (concerning disclosure) is still awaiting hearing before the Court. The third was heard in Belfast and established that the Commission was right to have understood that without some fresh factor or exceptional circumstances a reference cannot be based on issues that have been raised during an application for an extension of time in which to appeal *(R (on the application of McCrory) v CCRC* [2007] NIQB 93).

The remaining nine challenges stood unresolved at 31 March 2008, either at the pre-action stage or awaiting an indication from the Court as to whether permission to proceed would be granted.

One case of particular importance heard during 2007 was *R (on the application of Dowsett) v CCRC* [2007] EWHC Admin 1923, which made it clear that the Commission must still apply its usual test to the merits of an application even when that application is based on a finding by the

[1]Parliamentary Commissioner Order 2007 (SI 2007 / 3470)

European Court of Human Rights that the applicant's Article 6 right to a fair trial had been breached. In other words, a breach of Article 6 does not necessarily mean the conviction is unsafe.

The number of complaints and judicial reviews is not a very precise measure of the quality of the service provided. The nature of our work means applicants may be unhappy simply because their case is not referred. Therefore, Key Performance Indicator 5 (see page 32) looks at the number of cases re-opened as a proportion of complaints and pre-action protocol letters resolved and judicial reviews heard. The first target was for fewer than three cases to be re-opened, less than 4% of the total number of complaints/letters/reviews. Performance was better than target, with just two re-opened, 2.6% of the total number of complaints/letters/reviews.

The second target was that the number of complaints otherwise upheld should be fewer than seven and less than 9.5% of the total number of complaints resolved. Performance was again better than the target, with just three complaints being otherwise upheld, 3.8% of the total number of complaints resolved.

Resources

People

The Commission has not replaced Case Review Managers (CRMs) as they have left over the year, owing to budget constraints. As at 31 March 2008, there were 43 CRMs, compared with 47 last year. Other roles that became vacant were reviewed and filled only where essential.

Our target for staff absence, as set out in Key Performance Indicator 8 (see page 33), was that sickness absence should be fewer than nine days per full-time equivalent for the year, and other absence (other than for annual leave, public holidays, unpaid leave and sabbaticals – which includes, for example, compassionate leave) fewer than three days per annum. The actual figures were 11 days sickness absence and five days other. The average sickness absence figure was raised by a small, but higher than usual, number of staff on long-term sickness. The Commission is reviewing its sickness absence policy and has proactive return-to-work programmes in place.

Our target for staff turnover (excluding Commissioners), as set out in Key Performance Indicator 9 (see page 33), was that the percentage of staff leaving the Commission should be between 5% and 12%. It was 12.9% (compared with 7.9% last year) and the Commission now has a headcount (full-time equivalent) of 84 (excluding Commissioners), the lowest since March 2000.

The Commission plans to bring in an objective job evaluation system aligned to a new pay and grading structure in 2008/09. The aim is to ensure that all staff are paid fairly for the work they do. The initial job evaluation process was completed during this year. Work also started on developing a disability equality scheme.

Training and development remained important and the Commission continued to provide legal updates and other training for case reviewers. A further programme of skills training is being developed.

Environment

The Commission continues to review and improve its practices to achieve a minimal adverse impact on the environment wherever possible.

IT and security

During the year, the Commission framed its new five-year IT strategy for the period 2007-12. One of the main items in the strategy is renewal of our hardware and updating of major software applications. The opportunity will be taken to explore whether replacing our conventional client-server model with newer technology such as thin client or virtual desktops/servers would yield cost savings. Other work completed in the year included upgrading HOLMES2, which enables us to view data from major police investigations, and building a virtual development environment to help us to deploy updates to the system with minimal risk and disruption to users. A planned upgrade of Vectus, our case management system, had to be deferred because of timing difficulties.

A full review of our security arrangements was started during the year, but the scale of the project had been underestimated and this will now be completed during 2008-09.

Finance

The Commission is funded entirely by means of Grant in Aid from the Ministry of Justice, which is a cash grant. However, financial control is exercised by means of delegated Departmental Expenditure Limits (DELs) which are calculated on a resource accounting basis. DEL is divided into near-cash resource DEL, non-cash resource DEL and capital DEL, each of which is a budget control. Virement between budgets is not allowed except from near-cash resource to capital with the consent of the Ministry of Justice.

At the time of writing the Commission is awaiting notification of its delegation for 2008/09 and is operating under an interim authority to spend. The delegation will contain indicative budgets for the second and third years of CSR2007 as well as the firm budget for 2008/09. The amounts shown in the table below are estimates based on previously advised indicative DELs.

A comparison of DEL figures for the previous, current and the next three years is shown below:

	Delegated DEL			Indicative DEL		
	2005/06	2006/07	2007/08	2008/09	2009/10	2010/11
	£'000	£'000	£'000	£'000	£'000	£'000
Near-cash	6,959	6,715	6,761	6,661	6,561	6,461
Non-cash	839	893	513	513	513	513
Resource total	7,798	7,608	7,274	7,174	7,074	6,974
Capital	163	56	95	100	-	-
TOTAL	7,961	7,664	7,369	7,274	7,074	6,974

An application made during the year to vire £60k from the near-cash to the capital budget was approved, and actioned in the Spring Supplementary. The delegated budget for 2008/09 and the indicative budgets for 2009/10 and 2010/11 will be used as the basis for the Commission's business and corporate plans which map the strategic direction of the Commission for the next three years, and the detailed activities, success criteria, projections and Key Performance Indicators for 2008/09. The plans will be made available on the Commission's website once approved. The principal risks and uncertainties which the Commission faces when planning and managing its financial resources concern the number and type of applications received, the Commission's ability to recruit and retain expert staff, the provision and maintenance of appropriate IT systems and the level of funding received. The Statement on Internal Control on pages 41-43 describes how these risks and uncertainties are managed.

The cash Grant in Aid received from the Ministry of Justice in the year was £6.83M (2006 £6.74M), consisting of £6.74M for the operating activities of employment and running costs and £0.09M for capital expenditure (2006 £6.66M and £0.08M respectively). In accordance with government accounting rules which require Grant in Aid only to be drawn when needed, the Commission aims to maintain its monthly end of period cash balances below £200k. This was largely achieved during the year, with an average end of month balance of £147k. The £200k limit was breached in one month as a result of misjudging the timing of a major payment.

Financial performance
The primary indicator of financial performance is expenditure measured against the delegated Departmental Expenditure Limits (DEL).

Revenue DEL is made up of operating expenditure and cost of capital, including the interest element of the increase in the pension provision, but excludes the unrealised loss on revaluation of fixed assets. The Commission's actual expenditure compared with DEL was as follows:

	2007/08			2006/07		
	DEL*	Actual	Variance	DEL	Actual	Variance
	£'000	£'000	£'000	£'000	£'000	£'000
Near-cash	6,701	6,641	(60)	6,715	6,957	242
Non-cash	513	393	(120)	893	478	(415)
Total revenue	7,214	7,034	(180)	7,608	7,435	(173)
Capital	155	95	(60)	56	81	25
TOTAL	7,369	7,129	(240)	7,664	7,516	(148)

*stated after virement of £60k from near-cash to capital

Actual expenditure in DEL format is reconciled to total operating expenditure as shown in the Income & Expenditure Account on page 46 as follows:

	2007/08	2006/07
	£'000	£'000
Actual revenue expenditure in DEL format	7,034	7,435
Unrealised loss on revaluation of fixed assets	25	30
Interest on pension scheme liabilities	(160)	(147)
Interest on dilapidations provision	(17)	(16)
Cost of capital	121	94
Operating expenditure per I&E Account	7,003	7,396

Both near-cash and capital were underspent by £60K. This arose largely as a result of the deferment of an IT project due to problems experienced in obtaining quotations and obtaining procurement strategy approval. As the funding for the project was only available in-year, the delays meant that the project could not proceed. The underspend on non-cash was inevitable as the amount of budget granted was far in excess of our requirements. Non-cash is not susceptible to being managed in-year.

Financial performance as measured by expenditure against DEL is shown in Key Performance Indicator 7 (see page 33). Although our near-cash expenditure fell within the control thresholds, this was not the case for non-cash or capital, for the reasons set out above.

Financial statements

The accounts for the year ended 31 March 2008 are set out on pages 46 to 59.

The Income and Expenditure Account on page 46 shows operating expenditure for the year of £7.00M (2007 £7.40M). Employment costs have remained constant at £4.84M in 2007/08 compared with £4.85M in the previous year. This is largely the result of a frooze on recruitment imposed as part of our strategy to reduce costs in anticipation of the reduced budgets in the following years.

Running costs for the year were down from £2.11M in 2006/07 to £1.85M in the current year. IT costs have contributed to this reduction as there were no major projects during the year, and our legal fees in respect of judicial reviews were modest.

Investment in fixed assets during the year was largely restricted to IT hardware, development and software, and totalled £87k. The net book value of fixed assets at the end of the year stands at £413k (2007 £614k).

This reduction in the book value of fixed assets, combined with the continued increase in provisions for pensions and dilapidations, has resulted in an overall negative balance sheet value at the end of the year of £3.55M (2007 £3.36M). The net liabilities largely fall due in future years, and will be funded as necessary from future Grant in Aid provided by the Ministry of Justice. As a result, it has been considered appropriate to continue to adopt a going concern basis for the preparation of the accounts. This is discussed further in the Accounting Policies note on page 49.

Compliance with public sector payment policy

The Commission follows the principles of the Better Payment Practice Code. The Commission aims to pay suppliers in accordance with either the payment terms negotiated with them or with suppliers' standard terms (if specific terms have not been negotiated), provided that the relevant invoice is properly presented and is not subject to dispute.

	2007-08		2006-07	
	£'000	Number	£'000	Number
Total invoices paid in year	1,948	1,874	2,218	1,859
Total invoices paid within target	1,827	1,671	2,140	1,756
Percentage of invoices paid within target	93.8%	89.2%	96.5%	94.5%

We aim to achieve a target of 95% of invoices (both by number and by value) paid within settlement terms, and we are disappointed that our performance is below this, and in fact is worse than last year. We are still experiencing problems with a small number of suppliers with unrealistically short payment terms (as little as one week), and our average for the year has been dragged down by periods when we were experiencing staff shortages and payment system problems. Strenuous efforts will be made during 2008/09 to rectify these deficiencies.

No interest was paid under the Late Payment of Commercial Debts (Interest) Act 1998.

Corporate

Planning and monitoring

Progress against our business plan objectives was monitored on a regular basis by the Senior Management Team during the latter part of the year, as the business plan was not approved until a late stage. For this reason, it was not considered necessary formally to communicate the plan objectives to staff. Commission Meetings were kept informed of performance against key performance indicators throughout the year by means of a balanced scorecard, which forms part of an integrated management information pack. Only minor alterations were made to the pack during the year as feedback on its format and contents was generally favourable.

The management information pack also forms the basis of our reporting to the sponsor unit. Operational meetings are held normally each month to discuss performance and other issues, and the Chairman has met occasionally with the appropriate director in the Ministry of Justice. However, no meetings have taken place at ministerial level.

A complete revision of the business continuity plan was started during the year, but pressure on resources has meant that this project has had to be extended into 2008-09. Nevertheless, substantial progress has been made in identifying and classifying risks, and testing of the final plan will take place later this year.

Wider contribution

The Commission strives to identify matters of law, practice and procedure from its casework that it considers should be reported to assist with improving the criminal justice system. Although it had been intended to conduct an evaluation of the systems we have in place to identify such matters before the end of the year, pressure of other work has necessitated this being pushed into 2008-09. We remain committed, however, to ensuring that lessons we learn on the causes of miscarriages of justice are communicated appropriately. We are also keen to ensure that the body of information we have from 11 years of casework can be used in the same way by others. To this end we continued through the year with researchers from the University of Warwick using our casework database on three separate projects - one looking at the use of expert evidence, the second looking at the role of the Commission and the third (funded by the Legal Services Commission) at the impact of legal representation on applications to the Commission.

Although pressure on resources did not allow us to accept any new research projects in the year, we shall be entertaining applications from other academics as the current projects reach completion i be constructed, resources permitting, once our new Head of Communications is in post.

Communications

The Commission continued to work to promote public understanding of its role and to engage with stakeholders.

All applicants were sent a feedback questionnaire and 370 completed forms were received over the year. In response to the question: "Was it easy to find out about us?", 69% stated it was either very easy or easy (compared with 68% for the previous year). Applicants were asked for suggestions on how to make it easier for people to find out about the Commission and their responses helped inform our communications plans.

A new questionnaire was piloted during the last quarter of the year, asking applicants (following completion of their cases) for their views on the service provided by the Commission, together with comments and suggestions for improvements. The results will be reviewed in 2008-09.

A website survey form was also launched and the results will be used to help guide a redesign of the website next year.

The Commission continued to issue press releases for each case referred. Other activities over the year included:

- Hosting (jointly with the University of Birmingham School of Law) a major conference, Miscarriages of Justice: Causes and Remedies, to mark the 10th anniversary of the Commission. Speakers included the Rt Hon Sir Igor Judge, President of the Queen's Bench Division and Head of Criminal Justice, and Sir Ken Macdonald QC, Director of Public Prosecutions
- Hosting an Investigations Conference, at West Mercia Constabulary's Headquarters, for around 80 external delegates from investigative agencies with which the Commission has regular contact. The aim was to provide an overview of the Commission's work and feedback on lessons learned. Feedback from delegates was very positive
- Continuing to run a regular forum for stakeholders. A meeting was held in October 2007 with representatives from the Criminal Appeal Lawyers' Association, the Miscarriages of Justice Organisation and South Wales Against Wrongful Conviction.
- Hosting visits from various stakeholders, including the University of Bristol Innocence Project, a group of forensic registrars from the Reaside Clinic and a solicitor carrying out research for an article about the Commission
- Speaking about its work at a number of conferences and events, including the Criminal Appeals Conference 2008 and the Criminal Appeal Lawyers Association Conference, and participating in the Goudge Inquiry into Paediatric Forensic Pathology in Ontario, Canada.
- Contributing to discussion seminars on Law Commission proposals relating to possible reform of homicide law and the work of the Forensic Science Advisory Council
- Updating and redesigning leaflets about the role and work of the Commission. These were sent out to all prisons and NHS secure units, together with posters, and are given out at conferences and events.

No visits were made to prisons this year but the programme is being relaunched in April 2008, with the aim of carrying out six visits over the next year.

An action plan to improve internal communication was developed following a staff survey the previous year. A working group of staff from across the organisation continued to provide ideas and input into both internal and external communication.

Future developments

Following the implementation of new ways of working, we have reported this year on the dramatic fall in the number of cases waiting to be allocated for review and on waiting times.

We see 2008-09 as a year to capitalise on the benefits of the new processes, focusing particularly on the time taken to progress and close cases. That said, however, we are faced with the challenge to maintain and improve on our position in light of budget reductions and the consequent freeze on the appointment of new case reviewers.

The Commission continues to look for ways of improving its processes to ensure we can be as effective and efficient in case review as we can possibly be, without impacting negatively on casework standards. In addition, an evaluation of the new processes implemented as a result of the Commission's internal review conducted in 2005-06 will be concluded in the forthcoming year.

As reported in last year's annual report, provisions in the Armed Forces Act 2006 giving the Commission jurisdiction over court-martial convictions and sentences is expected to come into force in 2009.

Non-executive directors

The day-to-day running of the Commission is the responsibility of the Senior Management Team which comprises two executive directors and which reports to the Chairman and the Commission regularly. In the forthcoming year, it is proposed to appoint two non-executive directors who will join the Commissioners on the board of the Commission and contribute to the strategic oversight of the Commission

Table 1: Commission referrals to the appeal courts 2007-08

Name	Referral date	Offence	Court of Appeal decision and date
W*	29 Mar 07	Buggery; rape [x2]; indecent assault [x11]	
K	1 May 07	Indecency with a child [x3]; indecent assault [x3] (S)	Q 28 Sep 07
MOSES, Tony	1 May 07	Being knowingly concerned in the fraudulent evasion of the prohibition or restriction on importation of Class A drug (S)	Q 17 Dec 07
ATTWOOLL, Michael	22 May 07	Murder [x2]	
RODEN, John	22 May 07	Murder [x2]	
FOSTER, Mark	23 May 07	Attempted murder	U 30 Nov 07
KEMPSTER, Mark	25 May 07	Burglary [x3]; attempted burglary	
C	13 Jun 07	Rape [x2]; indecent assault [x2]	Q 16 Oct 07
OSMAN, Abdullah	18 Jun 07	Failure to produce an immigration document	Q 11 Jul 07
FULTON, Kenneth	19 Jun 07	Indecent assault [x5]	Q 08 Oct 07
GEORGE, Barry	20 Jun 07	Murder	Q 15 Nov 07
HAMMILL, Martin	26 Jun 07	Unlawful sexual intercourse; indecent assault	
ASHMAN, Faye	4 Jul 07	Allowing a dog to be in a public place without a muzzle or lead [x3] (S)	Q 18 Oct 07 Blackfriars Crown Court
SAMUEL, Michael	10 Jul 07	Assault occasioning actual bodily harm; making a threat to kill (S)	Q 20 Nov 07
McINTOSH, Demoy	26 Jul 07	Rape	U 28 Feb 08
BOWSER, Clive	2 Aug 07	Arson; intimidation; theft, affray; possessing an offensive weapon; criminal damage (S)	Q 14 Jan 08
T	13 Aug 07	Indecent assault	
SMITH, Gordon	14 Aug 07	Making a false statutory declaration	U 13 Dec 07
EVANS, John	16 Aug 07	Murder	
STOCK, Anthony	4 Sep 07	Robbery	
ANDERSON, Thomas	20 Dec 07	Conspiracy to murder	
ROWE, Christopher	9 Jan 08	Possession of indecent photographs of a child (12 counts)	
JAMES, David	16 Jan 08	Grievous bodily harm with intent	
MELNICHENKO, John	16 Jan 08	Grievous bodily harm with intent	
RICHARDSON, Colin	16 Jan 08	Grievous bodily harm with intent	
GIGA, Zulfikar	11 Feb 08	Incitement to cause grievous bodily harm with intent. Threat to kill	
HODGINS, Gerard	14 Feb 08	False imprisonment	
MORRISON, Danny	14 Feb 08	False imprisonment	

* The referral of W's conviction should have been included in the 2006-07 Annual Report, but was not. The cumulative figure for referrals has been adjusted to take this into account.

Q – Quashed, or sentence varied   U – Upheld   (S) – sentence only

Table 2: Commission referrals heard by the appeal courts 2007-08

Name	Referral date	Offence	Court of Appeal decision and date
*GRAY, Paul	14 Nov 05	Robbery, possession of a firearm with intent	U 28 Mar 07
McELWEE, Mark	21 Dec 06	Burglary [x2]; breach of licence (S)	Q 18 Apr 07
SAKAVICKAS, Rolandas	31 May 06	Conspiracy to launder money	Q 27 Apr 07
REICHWALD, Stephen	31 May 06	Conspiracy to launder money	Q 27 Apr 07
SINGH, Gulbir Rana	31 May 06	Conspiracy to launder money	Q 27 Apr 07
EL-KURD, Ussama	31 May 06	Conspiracy to launder money	Q 27 Apr 07
MASUD, Umar	27 Apr 06	Conspiracy to import heroin	Q 3 May 07
AHMED, Bahktiar	19 Jan 07	Conspiracy to evade the prohibition on the importation of a Class A drug; conspiracy to supply a Class A drug	U 4 May 07
SABIR, Mohammed	19 Jan 07	Conspiracy to evade the prohibition on the importation of a Class A drug; conspiracy to supply a Class A drug	U 4 May 07
BEG, Mohamed Akram	10 Aug 06	Being knowingly concerned in the fraudulent evasion of the prohibition on the importation of a class A drug; conspiracy to supply a class A drug.	U 4 May 07
AHMED, Mumtaz	10 Jul 06	Importation of heroin	U 4 May 07
RYAN, John Martin	10 Jul 06	Conspiracy to supply heroin	U 4 May 07
VERNETT-SHOWERS, Michael	10 Jul 06	Conspiracy to import heroin; conspiracy to supply heroin	U 4 May 07
McCLOY, John	1 Jun 06	Robbery	Q 15 May 07
S	28 Sep 06	Indecent assault [x4]; rape [x4]	Q 8 Jun 07
ALLEN, Stewart	20 Jul 06	Indecent assault	Q 12 Jun 07
McMENAMIN, Charles	22 Aug 06	Belonging to a proscribed organisation [x2]; having a firearm with intent [x2]; conspiracy to murder; possession of a firearm and ammunition with intent; possession of a firearm; collecting unlawful information; communicating unlawful information	Q 19 Jun 07
MACKIN, Paul	27 Sep 04	Wounding with intent [x2]; conspiracy to supply drugs [x3]	U 28 Jun 07
GORE, Lisa	24 Oct 06	Infanticide	U 5 Jul 07
OSMAN, Abdullah	18 Jun 07	Failure to produce an immigration document	Q 11 Jul 07
AHMED, Rizwan	10 Jul 06	Conspiracy to import heroin	Q 18 Jul 07
AHMED, Nisar	10 Jul 06	Conspiracy to import heroin	Q 18 Jul 07
RAMZAN, Mohammed	25 May 06	Conspiracy relating to the importation and supply of heroin	Q 18 Jul 07
B	14 Feb 07	Rape; indecent assault	Q 27 Jul 07
FLETCHER, Joseph	22 Feb 07	Indecent assault	Q 31 Jul 07
K	1 May 07	Indecency with a child [x3]; indecent assault [x3] (S)	Q 28 Sep 07
FULTON, Kenneth	19 Jun 07	Indecent assault [x5]	Q 8 Oct 07
C	13 Jun 07	Rape [x2]; indecent assault [x2]	Q 16 Oct 07
KENNEDY, Simon	24 Feb 04	Manslaughter	Q 17 Oct 07 House of Lords[1]

Name	Referral date	Offence	Court of Appeal decision and date
ASHMAN, Faye	4 Jul 07	Allowing a dog to be in a public place without a muzzle or lead [x3] (S)	Q 18 Oct 07 Blackfriars Crown Court
SOLOMON, Dean	18 Dec 06	Rape [x2]; indecent assault; buggery; attempted buggery	Q 22 Oct 07
HESMER, Alan	19 Sep 06	Attempted indecent assault; indecent assault [x2]	Appeal abandoned 18 Oct 07
HASKAYNE, Trevor Anthony	25 Jul 06	Conspiracy	Q 31 Oct 07
GEORGE, Barry	20 Jun 07	Murder	Q 15 Nov 07
ESAT, Ozer	13 Mar 06	Conspiracy to supply a controlled drug	U 20 Nov 07
SAMUEL, Michael	10 Jul 07	Assault occasioning actual bodily harm; making a threat to kill (S)	Q 20 Nov 07
ROBOTHAM, John	19 Jan 07	Indecent assault on a male	U 27 Nov 07
FOSTER, Mark	23 May 07	Attempted murder	U 30 Nov 07
KENNEDY, Robert	21 Feb 07	Murder	U 12 Dec 07
SMITH, Gordon	14 Aug 07	Making a false statutory declaration	U 13 Dec 07
MOSES, Tony	1 May 07	Being knowingly concerned in the fraudulent evasion of the prohibition or restriction on importation of a Class A drug (S)	Q 17 Dec 07
BOWSER, Clive	2 Aug 07	Arson; intimidation; theft; affray; possessing an offensive weapon; criminal damage (S)	Q 14 Jan 08
HILL, Ronald	11 May 05	Murder	U 29 Jan 08
G	20 Feb 07	Indecent assault [x5]	Q 1 Feb 08
CLARKE, Ronald	4 May 05	GBH, conspiracy to pervert course of justice	Q 6 Feb 08 House of Lords[2]
McDAID, James	4 May 05	GBH, criminal damage	Q 6 Feb 08 House of Lords[2]
McINTOSH, Demoy	26 Jul 07	Rape	U 28 Feb 08

*The decision on Paul Gray's appeal should have been included in the 2006-07 Annual Report, but was not. The cumulative figures have been adjusted to take this into account.

[1] Simon Kennedy's conviction was quashed by the House of Lords. Kennedy's case appeared in the Commission's 2004-05 report as a referral upheld by the Court of Appeal. The figures have been adjusted to reflect the outcome in the House of Lords.

[2] The convictions of Ronald Clarke and James McDaid were quashed by the House of Lords. These cases appeared in the 2006-07 report as referrals upheld by the Court of Appeal. The figures have been adjusted to reflect the outcome in the House of Lords.

Q – Quashed, or sentence varied   U – Upheld   (S) – sentence only

Key Performance Indicators

KPI 1   Cases in progress

Purpose: Case reviews should be completed within a reasonable time. This KPI measures how many cases in progress are in excess of the benchmark completion time. **Definition:** The number of category B and C cases which were allocated more than 6 and 18 months ago respectively, and which have not yet reached the provisional decision stage, and the average age of these cases in months. **Calculation:** Recorded for the current period and for the last 12 months. **Frequency:** Monthly. **Data source:** Case statistics compiled from the case management system.

Plan and performance:

	Target number	Actual number	Target avge age (months)	Actual avge age
Category B	<20	31	<10	12
Category C	<30	30	<32	42

KPI 2   Age of next case for allocation

Purpose: Of considerable concern to applicants is the length of time they must wait before their case is allocated for review. This measure gives an indication of these delays. **Definition:** The average age (in months) of all cases not yet allocated, and the age in months of the next case to be allocated (shown separately for in-custody and at-liberty cases for categories B and C). **Calculation:** Recorded for the current period and for the last 12 months. **Frequency:** Monthly **Data source:** Case statistics compiled from the case management system.

Plan and performance:

[months]	Target age of next case	Actual	Avge age of cases waiting	Actual
Category A	<5	5	<3	3.07
Category B custody	<9	5	<5	2.79
Category B liberty	<21	16	<11	10.52
Category C custody	<16	6	<8	6.89
Category C liberty	<28	17	<14	6.67

KPI 3   Case completion times

Purpose: In order to provide an optimum service to applicants, cases need to be completed within a reasonable time, taking into account the circumstances of the case. The time taken to complete cases will of course vary widely, although benchmarks have been set for each category. **Definition:** The elapsed time in months between allocation and the sending of the Statement of Reasons. The calculation is made twice, once to the sending of the provisional, and again to the sending of the final, Statement of Reasons. Cases involving an Investigating Officer and section 15 orders (investigations on behalf of the Court of Appeal) are excluded. **Calculation:** Recorded for the current period and for the year to date. **Frequency:** Quarterly and annually **Data source:** Reports generated from the case management system.

Plan and performance: Cases completed within time frame:

	Target to provisional SOR	Actual to provisional SOR	Target to final SOR	Actual to final SOR
Cat A	75% within 10 weeks	51.1%	75% within 20 weeks	66.1%
Category B	65% within 6 months	53.3%	65% within 9 months	60.4%
Category C	50% within 18 mths	76.5%	50% within 22 mths	58.7%

KPI 4   Caseflow balance

Purpose: A high-level measure of the time it takes to process cases efficiently is whether overall case closures exceed case intake. If they do, then backlogs will be eroded. If they do not, then cases will begin to accumulate and waiting-times will be extended. **Definition:** The total number of cases closed at all stages minus the number of applications received. Applications include section 15 directions from the Court of Appeal. **Calculation:** Recorded for the current period and for the last 12 months. **Frequency:** Monthly **Data source:** Case statistics compiled from the case management system.

Plan: Monthly: >-20, 12 month: positive **Actual:** 12 month: positive by 103 cases

KPI 5   Complaints and judicial reviews

Purpose: The number of complaints and judicial reviews may provide a crude measure of the quality of service provided. However, the nature of the Commission's work means that applicants may complain or apply for judicial review simply because their case is not referred, rather than as a result of unsatisfactory service. **Definition:** 1 The number of cases re-opened as a proportion of complaints and pre-action protocol letters resolved and judicial reviews heard. 2 The number of complaints otherwise upheld as a proportion of complaints resolved. **Calculation:** Recorded for the current period and for the last 12 months. **Frequency:** Quarterly **Data source:** Records of official complaints maintained by the Complaints Manager and of judicial reviews maintained by the Legal Advisors.

Plan and performance:

	Target number	Actual number	Target rate	Actual rate
Cases re-opened	<3	2	<4%	2.6%
Other	<7	3	<9½%	3.8%

KPI 6	Referral conclusions

Purpose: The proportion of referrals which result in a conviction being quashed or a sentence varied is a measure of our interpretation of the 'real possibility' test. **Definition:** The number of referrals in which judgment has been given in the period which have resulted in a quashed conviction or varied sentence as a proportion of the total number of referrals heard in the period. **Calculation:** Recorded for the 12 months to date and cumulative. **Frequency:** Quarterly **Data source:** Judgments delivered by the Court of Appeal.

Plan: >60% and <80%. Actual 65% for the 12 months, with a cumulative figure of 70%. Both figures are within the target range.

KPI 7	Expenditure against budget

Purpose: The Commission is required to operate within its delegated budget. A key indicator of financial management is the extent to which expenditure in the period is aligned with the delegated budget. Whilst overspends are not permitted, efficient use of resources requires that the budget available is fully utilised. **Definition:** Total expenditure less delegated budget, based on DEL and measured separately for resource near-cash, resource non-cash and capital, expressed as an amount and as a percentage of budget. **Calculation:** Forecast for the year to date. **Frequency:** Monthly. **Data source:** Management accounts.

Plan and performance:

	Amount £000			Budget %		
	Target		Actual	Target		Actual
Resource:						
Near-cash	0	-135	-60	0	-2	-0.9
Non-cash	0	-15	-121	0	-2	-23.6
Capital	0	-15	-60	0	-12½	-38.7

KPI 8	Staff absence

Purpose: The extent to which staff and Commissioners are absent affects the Commission's productivity and its ability to achieve its casework targets. **Definition:** The aggregate number of days of employee and Commissioner absence (other than for normal annual leave, public holidays, unpaid leave and sabbaticals), divided by the full-time equivalent number of employees and Commissioners, recorded separately for sickness absence and other causes of absence. **Calculation:** Recorded for the current period and for the year to date. **Frequency:** Monthly **Data source:** Internally generated data based on personnel records.

Plan: Sickness absence: < 9 days per annum Other: <3 days per annum
Actual Sickness absence: 11 days per annum Other: 5 days per annum.

KPI 9	Staff turnover

Purpose: The recruitment and retention of high-calibre staff is critical to the Commission's achieving its casework targets. **Definition:** Number of employees leaving the Commission during the period, expressed as a percentage of all employees (using FTE). **Calculation:** Recorded for the current period and for the year to date. **Frequency:** Quarterly **Data source:** Internally generated data based on personnel records.

Plan: < 12% and >5%. Actual 12.9%

Section
Two

Remuneration
Report

Remuneration policy

The remuneration of Commissioners is set by the Secretary of State for Justice, taking account of the recommendations of the Review Body on Senior Salaries. The Review Body takes account of the evidence it receives about wider economic considerations and the affordability of its recommendations, as well as factors such as the need to recruit, retain, and motivate staff and the Government's inflation target.

Further information about the work of the Review Body can be found at www.ome.uk.com.

Although Commissioners are appointed with different weekly time commitments, all Commissioners, with the exception of the Chairman, are paid salaries at the same full-time equivalent rate.

Salaries of senior management and advisers are set by the Remuneration Committee, which is made up of the Chairman, three other Commissioners and the Principal Director. The Committee takes into account Treasury pay growth limits, affordability, and performance in determining annual salary increases.

Service contracts

Commissioners are appointed by The Queen on the recommendation of the Prime Minister, one of whom is appointed by The Queen as Chairman. Appointments may be full-time or part-time, and are for a fixed period of not longer than five years. Retiring Commissioners are eligible for re-appointment, provided that no person may hold office for a continuous period which is longer than 10 years.

Senior management are employed on permanent contracts of employment. The normal retirement age is 65, although pensionable age remains as 60. Early termination, other than for misconduct, would result in the individual receiving compensation as set out in the Civil Service Compensation Scheme.

Salary and pension entitlements

The following sections provide details of the remuneration and pension interests of the Commissioners and the senior management team. These details have been subject to audit.

	2007-08		2006-07	
	Salary £k	Benefits-in-kind to nearest £100	Salary £k	Benefits-in-kind to nearest £100
Professor Graham Zellick – Chairman[1]	95 – 100	-	140 – 145	-
Mr Michael Allen	85 – 90	-	80 – 85	-
Ms Penelope Barrett	85 – 90	-	80 – 85	8,600
Mr Laurence Elks [to 31.12.06]	-	-	40 – 45	8,200
Mr Mark Emerton	50 – 55	17,200	45 – 50	17,000
Mr James England [from 01.11.06]	85 – 90	-	35 – 40	-
Mr Anthony Foster [to 31.12.06]	-	-	65 – 70	-
Miss Julie Goulding [from 01.01.07]	85 – 90	14,600	20 – 25	-
Mr David Jessel	60 – 65	6,300	55 – 60	15,500
Mr Alastair MacGregor	85 – 90	-	80 – 85	-
Dr James MacKeith [to 31.12.06]	-	-	25 – 30	6,000
Mr Ian Nichol[2]	40 – 45	-	60 – 65	-
Mr Karamjit Singh [to 31.12.06]	-	-	30 – 35	-
Mr Baden Skitt [to 31.12.06]	-	-	60 – 65	14,000
Mr Ewen Smith [from 01.11.06]	85 – 90	-	35 – 40	-
Mr John Weeden	70 – 75	-	65 – 70	-
Mr Colin Albert – Principal Director and Director of Finance & IT	70 – 75	-	65 – 70	-
Miss Karen Kneller – Director of Casework	60 – 65	-	60 – 65	-
Mr Peter Wilkinson – Director of Administration & HR [to 31.03.07]	-	-	45 – 50	-

'Salary' includes gross salary or remuneration.

The monetary value of benefits-in-kind covers any benefits provided by the Commission and treated by the Inland Revenue as a taxable emolument. Benefits received by Commissioners relate to costs incurred to enable part-time Commissioners to work in the Commission's office in Birmingham and relocation expenses.

[1]Prof Zellick became part-time (0.6 FTE) from 01.01.07
[2]Mr Nichol reduced his hours from 0.8 FTE to 0.5 FTE from 01.01.07

Pension benefits

	Real increase in pension and related lump sum at age 60 (bands of £2½k)	Total accrued pension at age 60 at 31/3/08 and related lump sum (bands of £2½k)	CETV at 31/3/07 to nearest £k	CETV at 31/3/08 to nearest £k	Real increase in CETV to nearest £k
Prof Graham Zellick - Chairman	0-2.5	5-7.5	117	152	17
Mr Michael Allen	0-2.5	7.5-10	95	131	19
Ms Penelope Barrett	0-2.5	5-7.5	55	86	19
Mr Mark Emerton	0-2.5 plus 0-2.5 lump sum	2.5-5 plus 10-12.5 lump sum	46	64	10
Mr James England	0-2.5	0-2.5	3	25	19
Miss Julie Goulding	0-2.5	0-2.5	3	25	19
Mr David Jessel	0-2.5 plus 0-2.5 lump sum	5-7.5 plus 15-17.5 lump sum	119	142	16
Mr Alastair MacGregor	2.0-2.5	7.5-10.0	94	147	27
Mr Ian Nichol	0-2.5	2.5-5	59	80	10
Mr Ewen Smith	0-2.5	0-2.5	3	32	25
Mr John Weeden	0-2.5	5-7.5	99	134	20
Mr Colin Albert - Principal Director and Director of Finance & IT	0-2.5	2.5-5	42	70	19
Miss Karen Kneller - Director of Casework	0-2.5 plus 0-2.5 lump sum	15-17.5 plus 45-47.5 lump sum	215	261	8

Owing to certain factors being incorrect in last year's CETV calculator provided by the Cabinet Office there may be a slight difference between the final period CETV for 2006-07 and the start of period CETV for 2007-08.

The real increase in CETV for certain individuals includes additional contributions made by the individual to buy added years as well as the normal contributions from the Commission. Commissioners may choose pension arrangements broadly by analogy with the Principal Civil Service Pension Schemes and are entitled to receive such benefits from their date of appointment.

Commissioners' pension arrangements are unfunded, and the Commission is responsible for paying retirement benefits as they fall due. Contributions are paid by Commissioners at the rate of 1.5% and 3.5% of pensionable earnings respectively depending on whether the individual's scheme is by analogy to the classic or premium/classic plus PCSPS schemes. Pension benefits to staff are provided through the Principal Civil Service pension arrangements. Scheme members contribute 1.5% of salary to classic and 3.5% of salary to premium and to classic plus. A Cash Equivalent Transfer Value (CETV) is the actuarially assessed capitalised value of the pension scheme benefits accrued by a member at a particular point in time. The benefits valued are members' accrued benefits and any contingent spouse's pension payable from the scheme. A CETV is a payment made by a pension scheme or arrangement to secure pension benefits in another pension scheme or arrangement when the member leaves a scheme and chooses to transfer the benefits accrued in their former scheme. The CETV figures include the value of any pension benefit in another scheme or arrangement which the individual has transferred and for which a transfer payment commensurate with the additional pension liabilities being assumed has been received. They also include any additional pension benefit accrued to the member as a result of their purchasing additional years of pension service in the scheme at their own cost. CETVs are calculated within the guidelines and framework prescribed by the Institute and Faculty of Actuaries.

The real increase in the CETV reflects the increase in CETV effectively funded by the Commission. It takes account of the increase in accrued pension due to inflation, contributions paid by the member (including the value of any benefits transferred from another pension scheme or arrangement) and uses common market valuation factors for the start and end of the period.

Statement
of Accounts

Statement of the Commission's and Accounting Officer's responsibilities

Under the Criminal Appeal Act 1995, the Secretary of State (with the consent of HM Treasury) has directed the Criminal Cases Review Commission to prepare for each financial year a statement of accounts in the form and on the basis set out in the Accounts Direction. The accounts are prepared on an accruals basis and must give a true and fair view of the state of affairs of the Criminal Cases Review Commission and of its income and expenditure, recognised gains and losses and cash flows for the financial year.

In preparing the accounts, the Accounting Officer is required to comply with the requirements of the Government Financial Reporting Manual and in particular to:

- observe the Accounts Direction issued by the Secretary of State (with the consent of HM Treasury), including the relevant accounting and disclosure requirements, and apply suitable accounting policies on a consistent basis;
- make judgements and estimates on a reasonable basis;
- state whether applicable accounting standards as set out in the Government Financial Reporting Manual have been followed, and disclose and explain any material departures in the accounts; and
- prepare the accounts on a going concern basis

The Accounting Officer of the Ministry of Justice has designated the Principal Director as Accounting Officer of the Criminal Cases Review Commission. The responsibilities of an Accounting Officer, including responsibility for the propriety and regularity of the public finances for which the Accounting Officer is answerable, for keeping proper records and for safeguarding the Commission's assets, are set out in Managing Public Money published by HM Treasury.

Colin Albert
Principal Director and Accounting Officer
30 June 2008

Statement on internal control

Scope of responsibility

As Accounting Officer, I have responsibility for maintaining a sound system of internal control that supports the achievement of the Commission's policies, aims and objectives, whilst safeguarding the public funds and assets for which I am personally responsible, in accordance with the responsibilities assigned to me in Managing Public Money.

The Commission provides information regularly to its sponsoring Department, the Ministry of Justice, on financial and casework performance. Monthly meetings are held with the sponsor unit at which performance measured against key performance indicators and progress against the Commission's key objectives are discussed.

The purpose of the system of internal control

The system of internal control is designed to manage risk to a reasonable level rather than to eliminate all risk of failure to achieve policies, aims and objectives; it can therefore only provide reasonable and not absolute assurance of effectiveness. The system of internal control is based on an ongoing process designed to identify and prioritise the risks to the achievement of departmental policies, aims and objectives, to evaluate the likelihood of those risks being realised and the impact should they be realised, and to manage them efficiently, effectively and economically. The system of internal control has been in place in the Commission for the year ended 31 March 2008 and up to the date of approval of the annual report and accounts, and accords with Treasury guidance.

Capacity to handle risk

The lead on risk management is taken by me as Accounting Officer. Individual risks are assigned to named individuals, and I ensure that risks are reviewed on a systematic and regular basis in conjunction with the relevant groups and committees. Each review is endorsed by the Audit Committee and a report made annually to the Commission. In addition, the assessment and monitoring of risk is embedded in the Commission's project management processes.

The risk and control framework

The Commission has established a risk management framework which ensures its risks are properly identified, managed and monitored. Risks are identified for each of the Commission's key processes, for major projects being undertaken and for the Commission as a corporate entity. Risks are assessed in the light of their financial, operational and reputational impact and likelihood on the organisation. This assessment includes an indication of both the risks inherent in the Commission's work and the residual risk actually faced by the Commission after taking into account the measures which have been put in place to manage the inherent risks. Where additional action is identified as being necessary to mitigate the effect of risks, this is fed into the planning process.

The Commission's control framework is based on the review of regular management information, administrative procedures including the segregation of duties, and a system of delegation and accountability. This is supported by regular meetings of the Commission at which the Commission's strategic direction and plans are reviewed and performance against goals is reported.

Work to improve the Commission's business continuity planning processes was included in the Commission's business plan objectives for 2007-08. The necessary revision of our business continuity manual, business area checklists and incident management procedures was almost completed in the year. This part of the work will be concluded in the forthcoming year, and testing carried out to ensure our processes are robust. The framework continues to identify those risks over which the Commission has limited control. These are principally the level of case intake and provision of financial resource. The Commission uses its management information to plan for the uncertainties associated with these areas of risk.

The Commission has appointed Grant Thornton as internal auditors who operate in accordance with Government Internal Audit Standards. Their work is informed by an analysis of the risks to which the Commission is exposed, and annual internal audit plans are based on this analysis. The analysis of risks and the internal audit plans are endorsed by the Commission's Audit Committee and approved by me. At least annually, Grant Thornton provide me with a report on the internal audit activity in the Commission. Their reports include their independent opinion on the adequacy and effectiveness of the Commission's system of internal control based on the work undertaken together with appropriate recommendations for improvement. In their opinion, the risk management, control and governance processes within the areas covered by their reviews in the year ended 31 March 2008 were adequate, effective and sufficient to enable the Commission to rely on the internal control system. Both internal and external audits provide a service to the Commission by assisting with the continuous improvement of procedures and controls. Actions are agreed in response to recommendations made, and these are followed up to ensure that they are implemented.

Review of effectiveness

As Accounting Officer, I have responsibility for reviewing the effectiveness of the system of internal control. My review of the effectiveness of the system of internal control is informed by the work of the internal auditors and the staff within the Commission who have responsibility for the development and maintenance of the internal control framework, and comments made by the external auditors in their management letter and other reports. I have been advised on the implications of the result of my review of the effectiveness of the system of internal control by the Commission and the Audit Committee and a plan to address weaknesses and ensure continuous improvement of the system is in place.

I have previously reported that the Commission is unusual for an executive non-departmental public body in not having a chief executive, who would normally also be the Accounting Officer. The sponsor unit was initially of the view that this entailed significant inherent risks, but these have now been reduced to an acceptable level following my appointment as Principal Director and the implementation of changes to the purchasing authority procedures to ensure that there is no conflict between my role as Director of Finance & IT and my role as Accounting Officer.

Plans to expand the 'board' (which currently comprises the Commissioners) to include two independent members are now well advanced. The independent members will be able to bring an outside perspective and improve the balance of expertise across areas such as business planning, finance, risk and performance management. This expansion of the 'board' complements the appointment at the beginning of 2007 of an independent chair of the Audit Committee, and will further strengthen the governance arrangements of the Commission.

During the year, vulnerabilities in our IT network were discovered as part of routine testing to ensure compliance with government security accreditation standards. These were second level vulnerabilities, and it is not thought that our information was at serious risk as a result. The vulnerabilities have nevertheless since been addressed, and we are confident that re-testing will reveal full compliance.

Colin Albert
Principal Director and Accounting Officer
30 June 2008

The certificate and report of the Comptroller and Auditor General to the Houses of Parliament

I certify that I have audited the financial statements of the Criminal Cases Review Commission for the year ended 31 March 2008 under the Criminal Appeal Act 1995. These comprise the Income and Expenditure Account, the Balance Sheet, the Cash Flow Statement and Statement of Total Recognised Gains and Losses and the related notes. These financial statements have been prepared under the accounting policies set out within them. I have also audited the information in the Remuneration Report that is described in that report as having been audited.

Respective responsibilities of the Commission, Accounting Officer and auditor

The Commission and Accounting Officer are responsible for preparing the Annual Report, the Remuneration Report and the financial statements in accordance with the Criminal Appeal Act 1995 and directions made thereunder by the Secretary of State with the consent of HM Treasury and for ensuring the regularity of financial transactions. These responsibilities are set out in the Statement of the Commission's and Accounting Officer's Responsibilities.

My responsibility is to audit the financial statements and the part of the remuneration report to be audited in accordance with relevant legal and regulatory requirements, and with International Standards on Auditing (UK and Ireland).

I report to you my opinion as to whether the financial statements give a true and fair view and whether the financial statements and the part of the Remuneration Report to be audited have been properly prepared in accordance with the Criminal Appeal Act 1995 and directions made thereunder by the Secretary of State with the consent of HM Treasury. I report to you whether, in my opinion, the information, which comprises the Directors' Report, Review of the year and performance, Casework, Resources and Corporate, included in the Annual Report is consistent with the financial statements. I also report whether in all material respects the expenditure and income have been applied to the purposes intended by Parliament and the financial transactions conform to the authorities which govern them.

In addition, I report to you if the Criminal Cases Review Commission has not kept proper accounting records, if I have not received all the information and explanations I require for my audit, or if information specified by HM Treasury regarding remuneration and other transactions is not disclosed.

I review whether the Statement on Internal control reflects the Criminal Cases Review Commission's compliance with HM Treasury's guidance, and I report if it does not. I am not required to consider whether this statement covers all risks and controls, or form an opinion on the effectiveness of Commission's corporate governance procedures or its risk and control procedures.

I read the other information contained in the Annual Report and consider whether it is consistent with the audited financial statements. This other information comprises the Chairman's foreword and How we work. I consider the implications for my report if I become aware of any apparent misstatements or material inconsistencies with the financial statements. My responsibilities do not extend to any other information.

Basis of audit opinions

I conducted my audit in accordance with International Standards on Auditing (UK and Ireland) issued by the Auditing Practices Board. My audit includes examination, on a test basis, of evidence relevant to the amounts, disclosures and regularity of financial transactions included in the financial statements and the part of the Remuneration Report to be audited. It also includes an assessment of the significant estimates and judgments made by the Commission and Accounting Officer in the preparation of the financial statements, and of whether the accounting policies are most appropriate to the Criminal Cases Review Commission's circumstances, consistently applied and adequately disclosed.

I planned and performed my audit so as to obtain all the information and explanations which I considered necessary in order to provide me with sufficient evidence to give reasonable assurance that the financial statements and the part of the Remuneration Report to be audited are free from material misstatement, whether caused by fraud or error, and that in all material respects the expenditure and income have been applied to the purposes intended by Parliament and the financial transactions conform to the authorities which govern them. In forming my opinion I also evaluated the overall adequacy of the presentation of information in the financial statements and the part of the Remuneration Report to be audited.

Opinions

In my opinion:

- the financial statements give a true and fair view, in accordance with the Criminal Appeal Act 1995 and directions made thereunder by the Secretary of State with the consent of HM Treasury, of the state of the Commission's affairs as at 31 March 2008 and of its net expenditure for the year then ended;
- the financial statements and the part of the Remuneration Report to be audited have been properly prepared in accordance with the Criminal Appeal Act 1995 and directions made thereunder by the Secretary of State with the consent of HM Treasury; and
- information, which comprises the Directors' Report, Review of the year and performance, Casework, Resources and Corporate included in the Annual Report, is consistent with the financial statements.

Opinion on Regularity

In my opinion, in all material respects the expenditure and income have been applied to the purposes intended by Parliament and the financial transactions conform to the authorities which govern them.

Report

I have no observations to make on these financial statements.

(Signed) T J Burr
Comptroller and Auditor General
National Audit Office, 151 Buckingham Palace Road, Victoria, London SW1W 9SS
4 July 2008

Income and expenditure account
For the year ended 31 March 2008

	Note	2007-08 £000s	2006-07 £000s
Employment costs	3	4,843	4,849
Running costs	5	1,852	2,108
Depreciation & amortisation	6, 7	283	408
Unrealised loss on revaluation of fixed assets	6, 7	25	31
Operating expenditure		7,003	7,396
Interest receivable		(15)	(12)
Interest on pension scheme liabilities	4	160	147
Interest on dilapidations provision	10	17	16
Notional cost of capital		(121)	(94)
Net expenditure on ordinary activities		7,044	7,453
Transfers from reserves	12	(299)	(430)
Notional cost of capital reversal		121	94
Net expenditure for the year		6,866	7,117

All activities arise from continuing operations

Statement of total recognised gains and losses
For the year ended 31 March 2008

	Note	2007-08 £000s	2006-07 £000
Revenue Grant in Aid	2	(6,735)	(6,663)
Net operating expenditure for the year		6,866	7,117
Unrealised surplus on revaluation of fixed assets		(12)	-
Grant in Aid for capital expenditure	2	(95)	(81)
Actuarial (gains)/losses on pension scheme liabilities	4	(127)	542
Transfers to Income and Expenditure Account	12	299	430
Total Recognised Losses for the Year		196	1,345

The notes on pages 49 to 59 form part of these accounts.

Balance sheet
As at 31 March 2008

	Note	31 March 2008 £000	31 March 2007 £000
Fixed assets			
Intangible fixed assets	6	53	83
Tangible fixed assets	7	360	530
		413	613
Current assets			
Debtors	8	246	287
Cash at bank & in hand	15	95	36
		341	323
Creditors: amounts falling due within one year	9	(267)	(395)
Net current assets/(liabilities)		74	(72)
Total assets less current liabilities		487	541
Provisions for liabilities and charges			
Pension provision	4	(3,562)	(3,437)
Dilapidations provision	10	(476)	(459)
Total liabilities		(3,551)	(3,355)
Income and expenditure account	11	(3,932)	(3,928)
Other reserves	12	381	573
Total Government funds		(3,551)	(3,355)

The notes on pages 49 to 59 form part of these accounts.

Signed on behalf of the Criminal Cases Review Commission

Colin Albert.

Colin Albert
Principal Director and Accounting Officer
30 June 2008

Cash flow statement
For the year ended 31 March 2008

	Note	2007-08 £000	2006-07 £000
Operating activities			
Net cash outflow from operating activities	14	(6,703)	(6,802)
Returns on investments and servicing of finance			
Interest received		16	12
Capital expenditure and financial investment			
Payment to acquire fixed assets		(84)	(119)
Net cash outflow before financing		(6,771)	(6,909)
Financing			
Capital Grant in Aid	2	95	81
Revenue Grant in Aid	2	6,735	6,663
Increase / (decrease) in cash	15	59	(165)

The Notes on pages 49 to 59 form part of these Accounts.

NOTES TO THE ACCOUNTS

1   ACCOUNTING POLICIES

Basis of Accounts

These financial statements have been prepared in accordance with the Accounts Direction given by the Secretary of State for the Ministry of Justice with the consent of the Treasury in accordance with paragraph 9(2) of Schedule 1 to the Criminal Appeal Act 1995. The Accounts Direction requires the financial statements to be prepared in accordance with the 2007-08 Government Financial Reporting Manual (FReM) issued by HM Treasury. The accounting policies contained in the FReM follow UK generally accepted accounting practice for companies (UK GAAP) to the extent that it is meaningful and appropriate to the public sector.

The financial statements have been prepared under the historical cost convention modified to account for the revaluation of fixed assets.

A summary of the Commission's principal accounting policies is set out below. These have been applied consistently throughout the year.

Going concern

The Balance sheet at 31 March 2008 shows net liabilities of £3,551k. This reflects the inclusion of liabilities falling due in future years which, to the extent that they are not to be met from the Commission's other sources of income, may only be met by future grants-in-aid from the Commission's sponsoring department, the Ministry of Justice. This is because, under the normal conventions applying to parliamentary control over income and expenditure, such grants may not be issued in advance of need.

Grant in Aid for 2008-09, taking into account the amounts required to meet the Commission's liabilities falling due in that year, have already been included in the department's Estimates for that year, which have been approved by Parliament, and there is no reason to believe that the department's future sponsorship and future parliamentary approval will not be forthcoming. It has accordingly been considered appropriate to adopt a going concern basis for the preparation of these financial statements.

Grant in Aid

Grant in Aid received for revenue expenditure is regarded as funding and is credited direct to the Income and Expenditure Reserve in accordance with the Financial Reporting Manual. Grant in Aid for capital expenditure is credited to a Government Grant Reserve. Each year, an amount equal to the depreciation and amortisation charge on fixed assets acquired through Grant in Aid, and any deficit on their revaluation in excess of the balance on the Revaluation Reserve, will be released from the Government Grant Reserve to the Income and Expenditure Account.

Fixed Assets

Assets are capitalised as fixed assets if they are intended for use on a continuing basis and their original purchase cost, on an individual or grouped basis, is £100 or more. Fixed Assets are valued at current replacement cost by using the Price Index Numbers for Current Cost Accounting published by the Office for National Statistics, except in their year of acquisition when their current and historical cost will not be materially different.

Any surplus on revaluation is credited to the Government Grant Reserve. A deficit on revaluation is debited to the Income and Expenditure Account if the deficit exceeds the balance on the Revaluation Reserve.

Depreciation and Amortisation

Depreciation or amortisation is provided on all fixed assets on a straight-line basis to write off the cost or valuation evenly over the asset's anticipated life as follows:

IT hardware / development	four years
Software systems and licences	four years
Furniture and office equipment	up to 10 years
Refurbishment costs	over the remaining term of the lease
Dilapidations	over the period remaining to the next break-point of the lease

Donated Assets

Donated fixed assets are capitalised at their fair valuation on receipt. Their value is credited to a Donated Asset Reserve. Each year, an amount equal to the depreciation charge on donated assets, and any deficit on their revaluation in excess of the balance on the Revaluation Reserve, will be released from the Donated Asset Reserve to the Income and Expenditure Account.

Notional Charges

In accordance with the Financial Reporting Manual published by HM Treasury, a notional charge for the cost of capital employed in the period is included in the Income and Expenditure Account along with an equivalent reversing notional income to finance the charge. The charge for the period is calculated using the Treasury's discount rate of 3½% (2007 3½%) applied to the mean value of capital employed during the period. The value of capital employed excludes the value of assets donated to the Commission.

Pensions

(i) Staff pensions

Staff are members of the Principal Civil Service Pension Scheme (PCSPS). The PCSPS is an unfunded multi-employer defined benefit scheme, and the Commission is unable to identify its share of the underlying assets and liabilities. In accordance with FRS17, the Income and Expenditure Account is charged with contributions made in the year.

(ii) Commissioners' pensions

Commissioners are provided with individual defined benefit schemes which are broadly by analogy with the PCSPS. These schemes are unfunded, and the Commission is liable for the future payment of pensions. The cost of benefits accruing during the year is charged against staff costs in the Income and Expenditure Account. The increase in the present value of the schemes' liabilities arising from the passage of time is charged to the Income and Expenditure Account after operating expenditure. Actuarial gains and losses are recognised in the statement of total recognised gains and losses, and taken direct to reserves.

The balance sheet includes the actuarially calculated scheme liabilities, discounted at an appropriate rate to reflect expected long term returns.

Operating Leases

Payments made under operating leases on Land and Buildings and Equipment are charged to expenditure as incurred.

Provision is made for the estimated costs of returning the leased office premises to an appropriate condition. The lease expired in August 2006, and the provision has been charged over the period of that lease to income and expenditure. On renewal of the lease, the estimated cost was revalued to the amount required at the first break point in the lease in August 2011. This revalued amount was discounted to the present value using the official Government discount rate for long term liabilities (GDP deflator - 3½%). The provision held at 1 April 2006 was increased to this amount. As the building alterations concerned give access to future economic benefits, a tangible asset was also created corresponding to the amount by which the provision was increased, in accordance with FRS12 "Provisions, contingent liabilities and assets". This tangible asset is amortised over the period to the first break point in the lease on a straight line basis, and the amortisation charged to income and expenditure account. The interest cost arising from the unwinding of the discount is also charged each year to income and expenditure account.

Taxation

The Commission is not eligible to register for VAT and all costs are shown inclusive of VAT. The Commission has no trading income and is therefore not subject to corporation tax.

2   GRANT IN AID

	2007-08 £000	2006-07 £000
Received for revenue expenditure		
Home Office* main estimate (Request for Resource 1, Subhead AD)	6,735	6,663
Received for capital expenditure		
Home Office* main estimate (Request for Resource 1, Subhead AD)	95	81
Total	6,830	6,744

*subsequently transferred to the Ministry of Justice consequent upon the machinery of government changes in May 2007

3   EMPLOYMENT COSTS

Commissioners	2007-08 £000	2006-07 £000
Salaries and emoluments	848	984
Social security contributions	98	128
Pension costs	249	162
	1,195	1,274
Staff		
Salaries and emoluments	2,828	2,754
Seconded-in, agency, temporary and contract staff	58	63
Social security contributions	210	210
Pension contributions	552	548
	3,648	3,575
Total employment costs		
Salaries and emoluments	3,676	3,738
Seconded-in, agency, temporary and contract staff	58	63
Social security contributions	308	338
Pension costs	801	710
Total	4,843	4,849

At 31 March 2008, the Commission employed 94 staff (2006 94). The average number of employees, expressed as full time equivalents, during the year to 31 March 2008 by category of employment was:

	2007-08	2006-07
Executive	9	10
Case Review Managers	41	41
Administrative support staff	38	37
	88	88

4   PENSIONS

(i) Staff

Pension benefits are provided through the Civil Service pension arrangements. From 30 July 2007, civil servants may be in one of four defined benefit schemes; either a 'final salary' scheme (classic, premium or classic plus); or a 'whole career' scheme (nuvos). These statutory arrangements (the Principal Civil Service Pension Scheme, or PCSPS) are unfunded with the cost of benefits met by monies voted by Parliament each year. Pensions payable under classic, premium, classic plus and nuvos are increased annually in line with changes in the Retail Prices Index (RPI). Members joining from October 2002 may opt for either the appropriate defined benefit arrangement or a good quality 'money purchase' stakeholder pension with a significant employer contribution (partnership pension account).

The Commission is unable to identify its share of the underlying assets and liabilities in these schemes. The scheme actuary valued the scheme as at 31 March 2007. You can find details in the resource accounts of the Cabinet Office: Civil Superannuation (www.civilservice-pensions.gov.uk).

For 2007-08, employers' contributions of £550,595 were payable to the PCSPS (2007 £538,837) at one of four rates in the range 17.1% to 25.5% of pensionable pay, based on salary bands. The scheme's Actuary reviews employer contributions every four years following a full scheme valuation. From 2008-09, the salary bands will be revised but the rates will remain the same. (The rates will be changing with effect from April 2009) The contribution rates are set to meet the cost of the benefits accruing during 2007-08 to be paid when the member retires, and not the benefits paid during this period to existing pensioners.

Employees can opt to open a partnership pension account, a stakeholder pension with an employer contribution. Employers' contributions of £10,788 (2007 £9,505) were paid to one or more of the panel of three appointed stakeholder pension providers. Employer contributions are age-related and range from 3% to 12.5% of pensionable pay. Employers also match employee contributions up to 3% of pensionable pay. In addition, employer contributions of £650, 0.8% of pensionable pay, were payable to the PCSPS to cover the cost of the future provision of lump sum benefits on death in service and ill health retirement of these employees.

(ii) Commissioners

Commissioners may choose pension arrangements broadly by analogy with the Principal Civil Service Pension Schemes and are entitled to receive such benefits from their date of appointment.

Commissioners' pension arrangements are unfunded, and the Commission is responsible for paying retirement benefits as they fall due. Contributions are paid by commissioners at the rate of 1.5% and 3.5% of pensionable earnings respectively depending on whether the individual's scheme is by analogy to the classic or premium/classic plus PCSPS schemes.

The scheme liabilities have been calculated by the Government Actuary's Department using the following financial assumptions:

	2007-08	2006-07	2005-06	2004-05	2003-04
Discount rate	5.30%	4.60%	5.40%	6.10%	6.10%
Rate of increase in salaries	4.30%	4.30%	4.00%	4.00%	4.00%
Price inflation	2.75%	2.75%	2.50%	2.50%	2.50%
Rate of increase in pensions (deferred and in payment)	2.75%	2.75%	2.50%	2.50%	2.50%

The following amounts have been recognised in the Income and Expenditure Account for the year:

	2007-08	2006-07
	£000	£000
Current service cost	286	253
Settlements and curtailments	-	(61)
Commissioners' contributions retained	(37)	(30)
Total charge to operating expenses	249	162
Interest on pension scheme liabilities	160	147
Total charge to finance and other costs	160	147

Actuarial gains and losses recognised in the Statement of Total Recognised Gains and Losses for the year and the previous four years are set out below, shown as an amount and as a percentage of the present value of the scheme liabilities at the balance sheet date:

	2007-08	2006-07	2005-06	2004-05	2003-04
Experience gains/(losses) on pension	3	72	83	(97)	(107)
liabilities	0.08%	2.09%	3.09%	-4.95%	-5.90%
Changes in demographic and financial	(130)	470	198	(96)	197
assumptions	-3.65%	13.67%	7.37%	-4.89%	10.85%
Net actuarial (gains)/losses	(127)	542	281	(193)	90

The movement in scheme liabilities is analysed as follows:

	2007-08	2006-07
	£000	£000
Present value of scheme liabilities at start of year	3,437	2,686
Current service cost	286	253
Interest cost	160	147
Actuarial (gains)/losses	(127)	542
Benefits paid	(194)	(191)
Present value of scheme liabilities at end of year	3,562	3,437

5 RUNNING COSTS

	2007-08 £000s	2006-07 £000s
Accommodation costs - general	599	605
Audit fee – external	16	15
Audit fee – internal	15	11
Information and publications	84	77
IT costs	486	672
Legal and professional costs	39	90
Library and reference materials	51	41
Office Services	107	121
Office Supplies	91	87
Case Storage	14	9
Operating lease payment for equipment	7	12
Payroll & pension costs	15	16
Recruitment	22	29
Relocation	22	22
Telephones	24	29
Training and other HR	60	67
Travel, subsistence and external case-related costs	200	205
Total	1,852	2,108

Accommodation costs include rent of £409,391 (2007 £428,079) on the premises held under an operating lease.

6 INTANGIBLE FIXED ASSETS

	IT Software Licences £000s
Cost/valuation at 1 April 2007	339
Additions	19
Disposals	(3)
Revaluation	(22)
Cost/valuation at 31 March 2008	333
Amortisation at 1 April 2007	256
Provided during the year	44
Disposals	(3)
Revaluation	(17)
Amortisation at 31 March 2008	280
Net Book Value at 31 March 2008	53
Net Book Value at 31 March 2007	83

7   TANGIBLE FIXED ASSETS

	Refurbishment Costs £000s	Furniture and Office Equipment £000s	IT Hardware/ Development £000s	Total £000s
Cost/valuation at 1 April 2007	802	419	1,338	2,559
Additions	-	8	69	77
Disposals	-	(1)	(34)	(35)
Revaluation	54	39	(89)	4
Cost/valuation at 31 March 2008	856	465	1,284	2,605
Depreciation at 1 April 2007	762	265	1,002	2,029
Provided during the year	9	38	192	239
Depreciation on disposals	-	(1)	(34)	(35)
Revaluation	54	27	(69)	12
Depreciation at 31 March 2008	825	329	1,091	2,245
Net Book Value at 31 March 2008	31	136	193	360
Net Book Value at 31 March 2007	40	154	336	530

8   DEBTORS

	31 March 2008 £000s	31 March 2007 £000s
Intra-government balances:		
Central government bodies	41	41
Local authorities	25	23
	66	64
Debtors	2	1
Travel loans to staff	11	21
Other prepayments	167	201
Total	246	287

9   CREDITORS DUE WITHIN ONE YEAR

	31 March 2008 £000s	31 March 2007 £000s
Intra-government balances:		
Central government bodies:		
Ministry of Justice	-	-
UK taxation & social security	125	143
	125	143
Trade creditors	75	211
Accruals & other creditors	55	40
Capital creditors	12	1
Total	267	395

10   DILAPIDATIONS PROVISION

The movement in the provision is analysed as follows:

	2007-08 £000s	2006-07 £000s
Provision at start of year	459	394
Provided in year: creation of tangible asset	-	49
	459	443
Unwinding of discount	17	16
Provision at end of year	476	459

11   INCOME AND EXPENDITURE ACCOUNT

	Note	2007-08 £000s	2006-07 £000s
Income and Expenditure Account at 1 April 2007		(3,928)	(2,932)
Revenue Grant in Aid	2	6,735	6,663
Net expenditure for the financial year		(6,866)	(7,117)
Pensions: actuarial gains / (losses)	4	127	(542)
Income and Expenditure Account at 31 March 2008		(3,932)	(3,928)

12 RESERVES

	Note	31 March 2008 £000s	31 March 2007 £000s
Government Grant Reserve			
Balance at 1 April 2007		573	916
Capital grant in aid	2	95	81
Depreciation transferred to Income and Expenditure Account		(274)	(393)
Unrealised surplus on revaluation of fixed assets		12	-
Unrealised loss on revaluation of fixed assets		(25)	(31)
Transfer from Revaluation Reserve		-	-
Disposed assets - NBV less proceeds		-	-
Balance at 31 March 2008		381	573
Donated Asset Reserve			
Balance at 1 April 2007		-	6
Depreciation / amortisation transferred to Income and Expenditure Account		-	(6)
Unrealised loss on revaluation of fixed assets		-	-
Transfer from Revaluation Reserve		-	-
Balance at 31 March 2008		-	-
Total		381	573

	2007-08 £000s	2006-07 £000s
Transferred to Income and Expenditure Account		
Depreciation / amortisation		
Transferred from Government Grant Reserve	274	393
Transferred from Donated Asset Reserve	-	6
	274	399
Unrealised loss on revaluation of fixed assets		
Transferred from Government Grant Reserve	25	31
Transferred from Donated Asset Reserve	-	-
	25	31
Cost of disposed assets less depreciation / amortisation		
Transferred from Government Grant Reserve	-	-
Transferred from Donated Asset Reserve	-	-
	-	-
Total	299	430

13 MOVEMENT IN GOVERNMENT FUNDS

	Note	2007-08 £000s	2006-07 £000s
Reserves at 1 April 2007	12	573	922
Reserves at 31 March 2008	12	381	573
Decrease in reserves		(192)	(349)
Net expenditure for the financial year	11	(6,866)	(7,117)
Revenue Grant in Aid	2	6,735	6,663
Actuarial losses on pension scheme liabilities	4	127	(542)
Decrease in government funds		(196)	(1,345)

14 RECONCILIATION OF THE OPERATING DEFICIT TO THE NET CASH (OUTFLOW) FROM OPERATING ACTIVITIES

	Note	2007-08 £000s	2006-07 £000s
Operating expenditure		(7,003)	(7,396)
Depreciation and amortisation	6, 7	283	408
Unrealised loss on revaluation of fixed assets	6, 7	25	30
Decrease in debtors		41	17
(Decrease)/increase in creditors		(141)	138
Pension provision	4	286	253
Pensions in payment	4	(194)	(191)
Pension settlements		-	(61)
Net cash (outflow) from operating activities		(6,703)	(6,802)

The decrease in debtors shown above excludes a debtor of £388 for bank interest receivable (2007 £502) as interest receivable is shown after operating expenditure in the Income and Expenditure Account.

The increase in creditors shown above excludes capital creditors of £12,163 (2007 £1,164).

15 ANALYSIS OF CHANGES IN CASH

	2007-08 £000s	2006-07 £000s
Balance at 1 April 2007	36	201
Increase/(decrease) in cash	59	(165)
Balance at 31 March 2008	95	36

16 CAPITAL COMMITMENTS

At 31 March 2008, capital commitments contracted for were £474 (2007 £nil).

17 COMMITMENTS UNDER OPERATING LEASES

At 31 March 2008 the Commission had annual commitments under non-cancellable operating leases as set out below.

Operating leases which expire:	Building £000s	Equipment £000s	31 Mar 2008 Total £000s	31 Mar 2007 Total £000s
Within one year	-	2	2	1
Between one and five years	-	7	7	6
In more than five years	532	-	532	532

18 CONTINGENT LIABILITIES

There were no contingent liabities at the balance sheet date. Provision had been made in 2007 in respect of uncertainties regarding two pension transfers that were outstanding. Depending on the resolution of the uncertainties, the additional pension liability had been estimated to range between £269,000 and £682,000. One transfer has now been resolved, and the circumstances surrounding the other have changed such that a provision is no longer required.

19 RELATED PARTY TRANSACTIONS

The Ministry of Justice is a related party to the Commission. During the year ended 31 March 2008, the Ministry of Justice provided the Commission with Grant in Aid as disclosed in the financial statements.

The Revenue and Customs Prosecutions Office (RCPO) is an independent government department prosecuting major drug trafficking and tax fraud cases in the UK. As at 31 March 2008, a debtor is shown representing the recovery of costs in a judicial review brought by the RCPO against the Commission. This debtor is disclosed as an amount due from central government bodies in note 8 above.

During the year ended 31 March 2008, none of the Commissioners, key managerial staff or other related parties undertook any material transactions with the Commission.

20 LOSSES AND SPECIAL PAYMENTS

There were no reportable losses or special payments made during the financial year.

21 FINANCIAL INSTRUMENTS (FRS 13)

FRS 13, Derivatives and other Financial Instruments, requires disclosure of the role which financial instruments have had during the period in creating or changing the risks an entity faces in undertaking its activities. Because of the largely non-trading nature of its activities and the way it is financed, the Commission is not exposed to the degree of financial risk faced by business entities. Moreover, financial instruments play a much more limited role in creating or changing risk than would be typical of the listed companies to which FRS 13 mainly applies. The Commission has limited powers to borrow or invest funds and financial assets and liabilities are generated by day-to-day operational activities and are not held to change the risks facing the Commission in undertaking its activities.

The Commission is not therefore exposed to significant liquidity risks, interest rate risk or foreign currency risk.

22 POST BALANCE SHEET EVENTS

There are no post balance sheet events to report.

The accounts were authorised for issue by the Accounting Officer on 4 July 2008.

Printed in the UK for The Stationery Office Limited
on behalf of the Controller of Her Majesty's Stationery Office
ID5846403   07/08

Printed on Paper containing 75% recycled fibre content minimum.
Design by Homer Creative Photography by Roy Peters